J $9.95
921   Bauleke, Ann
He   Rickey Henderson

DATE DUE

FE21'92			
MR19'92			
AP 8'92			
AP17'92			
MY30'92			
JE23'92			
JY29'92			
AUG 02 '96			
NOV 07 '97			
JY 02 '01			
AG 09 '01			

DEMCO

Rickey Henderson

Record Stealer

Ann Bauleke

Lerner Publications Company ▪ Minneapolis

To my students Louis, Reggie, Sarah, and Ross,
who, like Rickey, are motivated by their pride

This book is available in two editions:
Library binding by Lerner Publications Company
Soft cover by First Avenue Editions
241 First Avenue North
Minneapolis, MN 55401

LIBRARY OF CONGRESS CATALOGING-IN-PUBLICATION DATA

Bauleke, Ann.
  Rickey Henderson : record stealer / Ann Bauleke.
    p.   cm.
  Summary: Highlights the career of one of baseball's most
proficient base stealers.
  ISBN 0-8225-0541-X
  1. Henderson, Rickey, 1958-   —Juvenile literature.
2. Baseball players—United States—Biography—Juvenile
literature. [1. Henderson, Rickey, 1958-   . 2. Baseball
players. 3. Afro-Americans—Biography.] I. Title.
GV865.H45B38   1991
796.357'092—dc20   91-7193
[B]   CIP
                                                                     AC

Manufactured in the United States of America

International Standard Book Number: 0-8225-0541-X (lib. bdg.)
International Standard Book Number: 0-8225-9597-4 (pbk.)

Library of Congress Catalog Card Number: 91-7193

1 2 3 4 5 6 7 8 9 10 00 99 98 97 96 95 94 93 92 91

Contents

The Greatest Thief

Several steps off second base, Rickey Henderson glances side to side. He digs the spikes of his left shoe into the dirt and crouches into a lead. Reminding himself to get a good jump, he concentrates on the pitcher. Everyone knows Rickey is going to run. People in the crowd cheer and jump to their feet. They waited all winter and through the first month of the 1991 season for this moment. It's the first day of May and Rickey is one base short of breaking Lou Brock's all-time career record of 938 stolen bases.

People in baseball say there are two ways for a pitcher to handle Rickey Henderson the base stealer: ignore him and concentrate on the batter or throw to the base again and again. They say Rickey will soon become bored and take off for the next base. If the pitcher and catcher are perfectly ready and very lucky, they might catch him.

On this day, Tim Leary is pitching for the Yankees and he chooses to concentrate on the batter, Harold Baines. There goes Rickey. His head is down, his arms are pumping, and his legs are chugging, kicking up dirt on the base path behind him. Near third base he launches himself airborne, like Superman, and slides headfirst. The third baseman has no chance to apply the tag. "Safe!" the umpire signals. The crowd roars. Rickey stands up, hoisting the base above his head in triumph. "It's all over," he says to himself. "I'm number one!"

Rickey gets stolen base number 939 on May 1, 1991, to break Lou Brock's career stolen base record.

Spring 1991 should have been the best time of Rickey's career. He had been voted the American League's Most Valuable Player for 1990. He was only three bases short of breaking the career stolen base record. But instead of being a time of anticipation and excitement, spring 1991 brought injury, conflict, and criticism.

Before the season began, Rickey refused to report to the Oakland A's spring training workouts in Phoenix, Arizona. He had become dissatisfied with his contract. By the spring of 1991, 36 major league players had signed contracts that paid them more money than Rickey was earning. He believed that the four-year, $12-million contract he had signed after the 1989 season was outdated. As the best player in the American League, he wanted the A's general manager, Sandy Alderson, to renegotiate the contract.

Everyone wondered when Rickey would join the team. A's manager Tony La Russa wanted Rickey in camp. He explained that Rickey's value to the team has nothing to do with the amount of money he makes. "What's important to me," La Russa told reporters, "is a team's feeling, and Rickey is part of the team."

With good-natured humor, the A's players tried to coax Rickey to training camp. They donated money to the Rickey Appreciation Fund—a large jar for collecting dollar bills. La Russa hoped the fund, even though it didn't contain anywhere near the amount of money Rickey wanted, would convey an important message to Rickey: "You're worth more than $3 million. We know it. We want you here."

Rickey arrived to spring training one day late. The distractions in camp were many. Few reporters asked Rickey when he thought he would break Brock's record, or if he thought he could win the MVP award two years in a row. Instead, the reporters mostly asked Rickey about his contract dispute. When La Russa finally told Rickey it was time to play ball, he was ready.

Many baseball followers believed Rickey would break the record in Oakland against the Minnesota Twins during the first series of the season, or maybe even in the first game. Lou Brock arrived to watch the event.

On opening night, Rickey came within a base of tying the record. But through the next two games, he seemed unsure of himself at the plate. "He always talks to himself in the batter's box," Twins catcher Brian Harper said. Yet this time Rickey's chatter seemed less confident. He coached himself. "See the ball, Rickey," Harper remembered him saying. "Maybe he was pressing because he wasn't getting on base," Harper said.

In the third game of the season, Rickey hit the ball and sprinted to first base. He suddenly stopped and hunched over his left leg. He had strained a muscle.

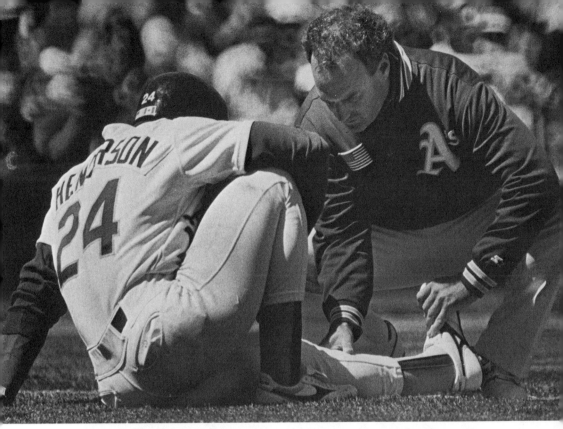

The 1991 season began badly for Rickey. He strained a calf muscle during the first week of the season and had to sit out of games for more than two weeks.

For the fourth time in his 12-year career, Rickey landed on the disabled list. He missed the next 14 games.

On his first day back in the lineup, Rickey tied Brock's record. The numerals 938 flashed on the Oakland scoreboard. The crowd cheered and a groundskeeper rushed out with a new base. Rickey kept the other base as a memento of the record. But in the next inning, when his left leg stiffened up again, La Russa and trainer Barry Weinberg took

Rickey out of the game. It would be another three days before he would break the record.

During Rickey's run for the record, he not only had trouble getting on base, he was also caught trying to steal four out of seven times. On the same day he finally broke the record against Tim Leary and the New York Yankees, he was nailed once in the first inning. After the game, Rickey said, "These last two bases were the toughest of my career. I think it was because of the pressure I put behind myself. Hearing the fans cheer, wanting you to go, you don't concentrate like you should."

The A's stopped the game when Rickey stole his record-breaking base so the fans could recognize his accomplishments. Rickey basked in the limelight.

The game was briefly interrupted while Rickey's mother, Bobbie, and Lou Brock joined Rickey on the field. Speaking into a microphone, Brock told Rickey: "You are the greatest competitor who ever ran the bases in the big leagues." When it was Rickey's turn to speak, he said, "Lou Brock is the symbol of great base stealing. But today, I am the greatest of all time."

His bold words annoyed some people, and he was criticized for saying them. But his statistics prove he is right. Brock set the record in 19 seasons. Rickey broke it early in his 13th season. As La Russa wished, Rickey finally measured his value by his achievements, not by the dollar amount on his contract.

The A's beat the Yankees 7-4 that day, and Rickey was caught stealing once more. But before his momentous day was over, 44-year-old Texas Ranger Nolan Ryan pitched the seventh no-hitter of his career. That night, a television reporter asked Ryan if his no-hitter stole the thunder from Rickey's milestone. "I don't think this will take away from what Rickey did," Ryan said. "Rickey did it in grand style—Rickey style."

Rickey Style

Rickey is 5 feet, 10 inches tall and weighs 190 pounds. His narrow hips and gnarled thighs are built for running. Even though he doesn't lift weights, Rickey's compact muscles are strong enough to withstand the pounding of his diving base stealing. But good base stealers rely mostly on technique and guts. The first time Lou Brock saw young Rickey run the base paths in the major leagues, he predicted Rickey would be the one to break his single-season record, set in 1974. Rickey, Brock said, had "base running arrogance." In other words, he wasn't afraid of getting caught. His cockiness comes from his confidence. He believes in his skills. His pride makes him great. But it has also caused people to dislike him.

Rickey has a big smile and eyes that crinkle up when he laughs. Waiting for a pitch, his eyes are still. But when he's on base, they dart back and forth, scanning everywhere, until they rest on the pitcher and watch for the best moment for Rickey to sprint for the next base. He always wants to steal, because he knows it psyches out the other team.

Rickey's style, as well as his abilities, distinguishes him from other baseball players. He is famous for his one-handed snatch catch in left field. Sometimes, after catching a fly ball, he snaps his glove in an arc, making the play look fancy. When Rickey bats, he might call a time-out just as the pitcher is about to deliver the ball. He might step out of the batter's box, smile at the catcher and say, "How you doing?" He drives pitchers and catchers crazy. But Rickey is just having fun playing baseball the way he learned the game while growing up and playing in the summer leagues in Oakland.

He was born on Christmas Day, 1958, in Chicago, Illinois. He was one of seven children. After he was two, Rickey never saw his father again. He was raised by his mother, Bobbie, but because his mother worked, he also spent a lot of time with his grandmother.

Rickey maintains close relationships with people he has known for years. His closest friends seem to be the same people with whom he grew up. He and his wife, Pamela, have been together longer than Rickey has been a major league baseball player. They have a daughter, Angela. Rickey's mother has been an important influence on his life.

Rickey hugs his daughter, Angela, at the Oakland airport at the end of the 1990 season.

When her husband left the family, Bobbie Henderson moved the family to Arkansas. About five years later, the Hendersons moved to Oakland, where they lived near a multi-sports complex. Rickey only hung around the facility until someone asked him, "Why don't you play sports?" Rickey had grown to love football while he was in Arkansas. The state is well known for its love of that game. Even though his older brother, Tyrone, loved baseball, Rickey dreamed of playing football in the NFL. "My brother taught me to play baseball because he didn't have anyone to play with," Rickey says. Tyrone threw baseballs at Rickey, forcing him to learn to catch. "I did it because I didn't want to be getting hit by the ball," he says. "I was an athlete. I could play. But I didn't like it."

When he signed up for Little League, he was still inexperienced at baseball. For example, Rickey was left-handed. Naturally, he threw the ball with his left hand. But everyone batted right-handed, so Rickey did too. He still does. Players who throw left-handed and bat right-handed are rare, and Rickey was one of only two nonpitchers to do so in the major leagues during the 1991 season.

In the summer leagues, Rickey played with Lloyd Moseby and Dave Stewart, who also grew up to be major league ball players. The summer league teams attracted an audience, and Rickey enjoyed the attention. "I think we thought we were entertainment to them," Rickey explains. "We learned how to play with a touch of style, a touch of class."

"Rickey hasn't changed since he was a kid," Moseby says. Rickey stills feels the game is for the fans, and he still strives to entertain them.

As a youngster, Rickey played against Dave Stewart, *above*, who has pitched in the major leagues since 1981, and against Lloyd Moseby, *left*, who has played in the major leagues since 1980.

When Tyrone was a senior at Oakland Tech High School, he wanted Rickey to try out for the baseball team. "He wanted me to be out there with him," Rickey says. "He was determined I was as good as anybody out there." Rickey was good, but he was only a sophomore. The coach decided Rickey should prove himself on the junior varsity team first. Rickey wasn't interested in the junior varsity team, and he stayed through the varsity tryout. The coach finally gave him a chance to hit during batting practice. When Rickey hit balls all over the field, he earned a spot on the team.

Rickey, in the baseball team's picture that appeared in the yearbook at Oakland Tech High School

This picture, also in the high school yearbook, appeared in the football section. Rickey was a standout running back.

Tommie Wilkerson, a small woman with a kind smile, was Rickey's godmother. She was also his high school guidance counselor. Ms. Wilkerson promised to give Rickey a quarter each time he stole a base. In 10 games, he stole 33 bases. His senior year, he stole 30 bases. He hit .716 one season and was pegged as the best player in the Oakland area by at least one pro scout. But in football, he rushed for 1,100 yards. He was still better known as a running back.

Scouts from both sports loved his abilities. By the end of high school, Rickey had to make a decision. He not only received more than two dozen football scholarship offers, he was selected by the Oakland A's in the fourth round of the 1976 baseball draft. When scouts from both sports tried to sign him—the A's to a minor league contract and the colleges to a letter of intent to play football for them—Rickey and his mother argued about which career he should pursue. Rickey preferred football. His mother, a great baseball fan, was afraid he would get hurt playing football. Finally, Rickey said, "Okay, Mom, whatever you want, I'll do." He thought she would give in to his wishes.

Ty Cobb, one of the first great base stealers, was known for his gritty play.

"I want you to play baseball," she said.

Rickey kept his promise and signed with the A's. They had been his favorite team while he was growing up, and Reggie Jackson (who played many years for the A's) was his favorite player. He decided to give baseball a few years. If he couldn't make it into the major leagues, he'd switch to football. "If I'd had the chance Bo (Jackson) had, I'd probably have played both sports," Rickey says.

The A's sent Rickey to Boise, Idaho, in the Northwest League, where he played short season A-ball, the first level of baseball in the minor leagues. He hit

.336. But more impressive, he stole 29 bases in 36 tries.

In 1977, his first full season as a professional baseball player, Rickey hit .345. His A-ball manager, Tom Trebelhorn, who later became manager of the Milwaukee Brewers, encouraged him to study films about other great base stealers. Because of his aggressiveness, Ty Cobb was Rickey's favorite.

As a result of Trebelhorn's encouragement, Rickey led the California League with 95 steals in 134 games and scored 120 runs. Trebelhorn teased Rickey, saying the reason he stole so many bases was that he became bored just standing on base, so he would take off for the next one. In one game, he became the fourth player ever in professional baseball to steal seven bases in one game. He was already making his mark. The fans loved Rickey's speed. They had so much fun with him that a match between Rickey and a race horse was planned at the ballpark. The horse won, but just barely.

Promoted to Double-A in 1978, Rickey's 81 steals led the Eastern League. The next year, in Triple-A, the highest rung on the minor league ladder, he hit .309, and stole 44 bases in 71 games. On June 23, the A's called him to Oakland and wrote him into the starting lineup for good. By the end of the season, he had hit .274 in 89 games and led the A's with 33 stolen bases.

During 1982, Rickey was tearing up the base paths. Here, he collects stolen base number 119, despite the efforts of Robin Yount of the Milwaukee Brewers, to break the single-season mark.

3

Stealing a Record

In order to steal, a player first has to get on base. For that reason, a good eye at the plate is a special advantage for a talented base stealer. With a good eye for seeing pitches as either balls or strikes, a batter can draw walks more often. A walk to Rickey is almost the same as a double. He often ends up at second base before the next hitter completes his at bat. Drawing 104 walks his second year in the minor leagues, Rickey demonstrated his eye for the strike zone.

Pitcher Ron Guidry once named Rickey Henderson the hardest player in baseball to pitch to. Rickey's batting stance is the reason. At the plate, Rickey crouches low, reducing his strike zone to only 10 to 12 inches. The strike zone is the space above the plate and within the area bordered by the batter's knees and armpits. "Stand up like a man," catchers and pitchers used to tell him. But Rickey didn't change. He could see the ball better from his unique stance. His .403 on-base percentage is proof enough that the crouch suits Rickey. On-base percentage is a statistic used to determine how effective a batter is at getting on base. Even though Rickey bats .293, he gets on base much more often because he can draw walks.

In 1980, his first full season in the majors, Rickey walked 117 times, second most in the American League. That same year, he stole 100 bases to break Ty Cobb's American League record for steals in a season (96). He became the first American League player, and only the third baseball player of all time (along with Lou Brock and Maury Wills, who played their entire careers in the National League) to steal 100 bases or more in a season.

The way Rickey stands at the plate gives pitchers nightmares.

The next year, in a strike-shortened season, Rickey stole 56 bases, scored 89 runs, and had 135 hits in 108 games to lead the American League in those categories. He experienced post-season play for the first time when the A's played the Kansas City Royals for the division title under a special play-off format. In three games and 11 at bats, Rickey hit only .182. But in the same number of games and at bats against the Yankees in the league championship series, he hit .364. Three of his four hits went for extra bases, and he stole two bases. Still, Oakland lost in its bid for a World Series appearance that year.

During the 1981 season, the Oakland outfielders began to draw notice as a unit. The three players—Rickey in left, Dwayne Murphy in center, and Tony Armas in right—played excellent defense together. Gradually, reporters began to focus more on Rickey's achievements. Baseball fans soon learned that Rickey had bought a block of 50 seats, called Henderson Heights, in the A's Coliseum. He donated tickets to children from the community. He referred to the children as "my kids."

The fans in left field cheered him when he ran to his position in the outfield. Most players avoid chattering with fans, posing for photographs, and signing autographs during the game, believing that it disrupts their concentration. But in Oakland, Rickey would wave, blow kisses, and talk to the fans. His teammates worried about Rickey missing the ball because of the fans. But Rickey said, "When the ball's not coming your way, you get bored. The fans keep me in the game."

From 1980 to 1982, Billy Martin managed the A's. His confidence in Rickey's talents played a big part in the direction of Rickey's career. It was Martin who encouraged him during spring training in 1982 to aim at Brock's record for the most stolen bases in a season (118). And yet, Martin wouldn't let Rickey run on his own. He had to wait for the steal sign from the manager in the dugout. Rickey loved to run, but Martin wanted to guard Rickey's body from too much wear and tear. Martin's insistence on calling for the steal caused the only conflict between him and Rickey.

The first two months of the 1982 season, Rickey averaged almost a stolen base per game. This blazing pace attracted the media. Reporters asked Rickey's teammates, managers around the league, and former ball players famous for their base stealing to comment on Rickey Henderson. One of Rickey's teammates at the time, Davey Lopes (who had the highest base stealing percentage in major league history), said, "He's much more daring than anyone I've ever seen. His desire to run is constant."

Others marveled at his headfirst belly slide. Feetfirst slides are more commonly used. Rickey learned the headfirst slide in the minor leagues from Michael

Rodriguez, a teammate. At first, he bounced all over the place when he dove into a base. He was tagged out several times that year when he slid over the base and couldn't get back in time. He had to learn to control his momentum.

Maury Wills found out that sliding feetfirst tears up base stealers' legs. Rickey's style of sliding is hard on his whole body. His hands, out in front of his body, break the slide. His chest pounds into the ground as he flies toward the base. His shoulders not only hit the dirt, but also collide with the infielder attempting to tag him out or make a double play.

Rickey slides into second long before Tim Foli can apply the tag.

Rickey's slides aren't always easy on the opposing team either. "He's hurt me more diving than anybody else ever did sliding," said shortstop Tim Foli, who played with the California Angels during the 1982 and 1983 seasons.

As Rickey's fame grew, his mental approach to base stealing was compared with those of other great thieves. For example, Lou Brock, who studied mathematics in college, took a scientific approach to base stealing. He knew that the ball takes 2.9 seconds under ideal conditions to travel from the pitcher to the catcher to second base. Counting his steps, he calculated a safe but daring lead off first base. Davey Lopes studied the pitchers. He memorized their movements and tried to learn clues to each pitcher's pickoff play. As for Rickey, he relied on raw speed. He simply tucked his head and ran as fast as he could. His ability to reach top speed in only two steps was one reason for his success.

During the 1982 season, Rickey's rush toward Brock's single-season stolen base record attracted swarms of reporters. It was the biggest event in baseball since 1974, when Hank Aaron broke Babe Ruth's career home run record. Rickey enjoyed the attention, and the reporters seemed to like him. His unique style on and off the field intrigued them. They found it noteworthy that he wore non-prescription glasses because, as he said, he could read better with them on.

Lou Brock, getting a good jump on the pitcher here, applied mathematics to his base stealing.

His teammates nicknamed him after actor Billy Dee Williams for his slicked back hairdo, and they sometimes teased him for his love of flashy clothes.

One part of the hoopla around Rickey's effort was a lingering controversy over *when* it is acceptable to steal a base. If a team was winning or losing by many runs, some people considered stealing to be a selfish act. They claimed that a ball player who tried to steal under those circumstances placed more value on individual statistics than on helping the team. Detroit Tigers manager Sparky Anderson was one of those people. He wondered how many of Rickey's stolen bases "meant something." In other words, he doubted that Rickey's steals helped the A's win games.

31

The Detroit Tigers gave up stolen base number 116, *above*, then number 117, but wouldn't give Rickey the satisfaction of breaking —or even tying—the record at home.

Near the end of August, the A's played a series against the Detroit Tigers in Oakland. Going into the final game of the series, Rickey needed only three more steals to tie Brock's record. He hoped to break the record at home for the fans, and his chances looked good. The Tigers were forced to use a third-string backup catcher, Bill Fahey, and Billy Martin believed Rickey's speed would get him to base before Fahey's arm could get the ball there.

In the first inning, with Jerry Ujdur on the mound, Rickey walked and promptly stole second and third bases for numbers 116 and 117. By the eighth inning, the A's led 3-0 and Rickey was due to hit. The noisy crowd grew louder. Fred Stanley, the A's shortstop, led off the inning. With a batting average of .186, he seemed unlikely to end up on base ahead of Rickey. But surprisingly, he drew a walk in four straight pitches. Many Oakland fans were suspicious. In order for Rickey to steal, the next base on the diamond would have to be empty. With Stanley on second, Rickey had no where to run. Had the Tigers walked Stanley to prevent Rickey from breaking the record at home?

If Rickey could steal second, he was just as likely to steal third for number 119. He hit a single to get on base, but with second base occupied, he had to stay put.

Even though Stanley had stolen only 11 bases in 13 years, he took a bold lead at second. Before long, Ujdur's pickoff throw caught Stanley off the base. Second base was open. Now, the same people who wondered if the Tigers had walked Stanley on purpose were wondering if Stanley had gotten himself picked off on purpose. With second base open, Rickey took off on the first pitch to the next batter. But the Tigers had called for a pitchout—a pitch intentionally thrown far away from the batter so the catcher can try to throw out a runner faster—and Rickey was called out on the play.

After the game, both teams were angry. Tiger Manager Sparky Anderson accused Stanley of allowing himself to get thrown out to clear the base for Rickey. Billy Martin accused the umpire of calling the out just to be known as the man who prevented Rickey's record-breaking steal. Although Rickey failed to break the stolen base record at home, he accomplished a different statistic that day. He tied Ty Cobb's 1915 record for the number of times caught stealing in a season (38). The next day, when the A's traveled to Milwaukee for a series against the Brewers, Rickey tied Brock's record with one steal in the game.

Undeterred by the controversy, Rickey ran the bases hard in Milwaukee and stole number 119.

While a dejected Robin Yount stays on the ground, Rickey picks up a souvenir.

With Lou Brock beside him, Rickey displays the base to the fans
at County Stadium in Milwaukee.

In the third inning of the second game of the series against Milwaukee, Rickey walked on four pitches. Pitcher Doc Medich threw to first base three times in a row. When he finally pitched to the hitter, Wayne Gross, Rickey took off. Catcher Ted Simmons, who had nailed Rickey several times during the season, this time had called for a pitchout. His throw reached second about the time Rickey's helmet flew into left field. "Safe!" the umpire signaled. As Rickey crawled up from the dirt, he pulled the base along with him, holding it proudly over his head. A groundskeeper delivered the base to Brock, who waited at home plate to congratulate his record-breaker. In an interview after the game, Rickey thanked his teammate, Dwayne Murphy, who had batted behind him all year and sacrificed his own at bat many times so Rickey could steal bases.

Even though Rickey broke Brock's record, he felt he had been distracted by all the hubbub created along the way. He drew 116 walks during the season, but he also struck out 94 times, and hit only .267. He hadn't hit below .300 since his rookie season. Worst of all, he was caught stealing 42 times, nearly doubling his previous high. Rickey said he was "overconfident and wasn't concentrating." When Rickey loses concentration, he also loses some of his aggressiveness. He made up his mind to improve his baserunning skills the next season.

Yankee Pride

In the minor leagues, Rickey had studied the techniques of Cobb and Brock. As a major leaguer, he was fortunate to have another great base stealer as a teammate. Davey Lopes, whose long major league career overlapped both Brock's and Rickey's, taught Rickey to rely not only on his speed, but also on his knowledge of the pitchers. For instance, careful study of a pitcher's delivery can be useful to a base runner. Sometimes one tiny gesture squeals on a pitcher, alerting the runner to a pickoff play, or telling the runner to expect a curve ball. A curve ball is a good pitch to run on because it reaches the catcher's mitt more slowly than some other pitches. If the base runner anticipates a curve ball, he can get a good jump on the pitch and increase his chance of beating the catcher's throw to the base.

Rickey's work paid off. He stole 108 bases during the 1983 season to become the first major league player to steal over a 100 bases in a season more than once. (Later, Vince Coleman would accomplish the same feat with the St. Louis Cardinals.) Best of all, he was caught stealing only 19 times during the season. The headlines for Rickey read, "Baseball's Best Thief."

Hall of Famer Willie Mays influenced Rickey's game in another area. Mays played outfield for 21 years with the Giants, first in New York, then in San Francisco when the team moved there in 1958. The most famous play Mays made during his career was a spectacular over-the-shoulder catch in the 1954 World Series. Most of the time, however, he used a basket catch, in which he caught the ball with his palms up at about waist level in front of his body, even though most players caught the ball above their heads.

Rickey wanted to do something different too—something that would set him apart from other players. He dreamed up his snatch catch. Rather than getting his glove into position and waiting for the ball to land in it, Rickey would wait until the ball had just about reached him. Then, in one fast, continuous motion, he would grab it with his glove. He practiced snatching the ball out of the air for a long time, but he was afraid to try it in a game. He didn't want to drop a fly ball.

The first time Rickey dared to use the snatch catch in a game, Oakland was playing the Chicago White Sox and the A's pitcher, Mike Warren, had a no-hitter going.

Rickey autographs a program for a young fan.

With two outs in the ninth inning, a fly ball sailed toward Rickey in left. He snatched it out of the air with one hand. After the game, his teammates told him, "If you'd dropped that ball, we would've killed you." But Rickey now *knew* he could make the snatch catch, and he began using it regularly.

After that, whenever he caught the ball the normal way, fans pleaded, "Rickey, please—snatch it." So he does it for the fans. "I love it, my kids love it," he said. He heard only one complaint from parents: "My kid tried your snatch catch—the ball hit him in the head."

Rickey enjoyed playing in Oakland, near his family and hometown fans. He had even bought his mother a new house near his own after the 1982 season. But a new dream quietly grew in his heart. Billy Martin had helped Rickey believe in himself. He once told Rickey, "You are a Yankee because you are the best." Rickey never forgot Martin's words. Because of his pride in his abilities and accomplishments, Rickey thought he might one day like to be a Yankee. That happened when he was traded to New York the winter after the 1984 season.

Every spring, the first day of the baseball season is a big event for the players and for the fans. But when he arrived at Yankee Stadium on opening day in 1985, Rickey had only one thing on his mind. He wanted to test his ankle. He had sprained it in spring training and was eager to find out if he could play in the starting lineup. The reporters had different ideas. They wanted to interview Rickey before his first official game as a Yankee. Rickey was more interested in checking out his ankle. He told the reporters he didn't want to talk. "They took it the wrong way," Rickey says, "and from that time, I was on the bad side of them."

Once a Yankee, always a Yankee. Billy Martin remained loyal to the Yankees, where he began his major league playing career in 1950. In the seven years from 1950 through 1956, when Billy played second base, the Yankees played in six World Series—winning five of them. Later, Billy coached the Yankees several times, bringing them to the World Series two more times. He coached Rickey in Oakland from 1980 to 1982, and then in New York during the 1985 and 1988 seasons.

Before Rickey could finally make his first plate appearance as a Yankee, his left ankle was heavily taped to help prevent further injury to the ligaments.

After missing the first 10 games of the 1985 season, Rickey had an outstanding year as a Yankee. He hit .314 and scored the most runs (146) of any player in baseball since Ted Williams (150) in 1949. He was the first player ever to steal more than 50 bases and hit more than 20 home runs in the same season. He did it with 24 home runs and 80 steals. Rickey was one of the best leadoff men in baseball, along with Tim Raines of the Montreal Expos.

In 1986, while Raines went on to win the National League batting title, Rickey reached a career high in home runs with 28. Hitting nine of those homers in the first at bat of a game, he set a new American League record. His 130 runs led the majors for the second year in a row. He also drove in the most runs ever in his career (74). "When I came up, I thought my job was just to steal bases," he said. "That's how I made my name. But gradually I found out how many different things I can do." He still led the league in stolen bases, however, with 87.

Rickey still considered base stealing to be a big part of his game. He wasn't about to stop. Several years later, Montreal Expos baserunning coach Tommy Harper told *Sports Illustrated* that "99.99 percent of base stealers lose their desire to be great base stealers after a while. They're different from hitters. They tire of every part of their body hurting every day." Harper says Rickey is different. "He's 31 years old, rich, famous, great—and he never lost the thrill of competing."

In 1987 there was great excitement in New York. The Yankees were in a pennant race. Even though their ace pitcher, Ron Guidry, didn't pitch until June and first baseman Don Mattingly, a .332 career hitter, was batting only .239 in May, the Yankees were at the top of the American League East. But along with the thrills of first place, the team felt pressure too. The Yankees were always supposed to be the best. Yet, they hadn't won a World Series in nine years. This year New York was determined to win.

Rickey, *center*, watches practice before the 1987 All-Star Game with pitchers Jack Morris, *left*, and Mike Witt. Rickey has played in the All-Star Game almost every year of his career.

In July, Rickey began to feel pain in his hamstring, the muscle at the back of his upper leg. He didn't know exactly what was wrong; he just knew something was wrong. The trainers said he had pulled his hamstring and treated it while he sat out a couple of days. But when he got back into the lineup, he complained that his leg was still too sore and that he couldn't run at full speed.

The Yankees became impatient. Without Rickey in the lineup, the team was slipping from first place. The media suggested that Rickey was faking the injury, that maybe he just didn't want to play. Rickey was shocked. "Can you tell me a baseball player, who is having one of his greatest years, doesn't want to play?" he asked some of the writers. "I'm on a winning team. I'm having fun. Do I want to sit on the bench and just watch? No, that ain't Rickey Henderson."

Finally, after he reinjured the hamstring while trying to steal a base, Rickey was placed on the disabled list for 15 days. Without him in the lineup, the Yankees lost three out of four games to the Kansas City Royals and were challenged by the Detroit Tigers for first place. When he came off the disabled list, he tested his leg. At first he jogged slowly. Nothing happened. But when he ran at full speed, the pain hit. Finally the Yankee's owner, George Steinbrenner, sent Rickey for special x-rays. The pictures showed a large tear in the hamstring.

Rickey's seven-year stretch of leading the league in stolen bases and stealing more than 50 bases ended, and the Yankees dropped out of the pennant race. The media never blamed Mattingly for his poor performance early in the season. They never blamed Guidry for his long absence from the team. But Rickey's bad start with the newspaper reporters on opening day in 1985 returned to haunt him. They blamed Rickey. The things written in the New York press hurt Rickey's pride even more than the injury hurt his leg.

Though the media continued to criticize Rickey for missing a game now and then, Mattingly defended him. "He needs days off," Mattingly said. "He runs around center field. The pounding he takes on the bases astounds me. I play first base and don't run, so I don't need days off. But he sure does."

When Rickey was criticized for sitting out games because he was injured or needed to rest, Don Mattingly came to his defense.

On June 20, 1989, the Yankees traded Rickey back to the Oakland A's. Because he had hit only .247 and stole only 25 bases so far that season, the newspapers wrote that Rickey was "washed up." His teammates disagreed. Mattingly said, "No one's played harder on this team than Rickey Henderson."

Even though he felt the pride of the Yankees and his own pride in himself, Rickey was ready for a change. "That pride," Rickey said, "made me say, 'I want to be a Yankee.' But then they tore my pride up."

In returning to the A's, where he began his career, Henderson was joining a team that had played in the World Series the previous year, and that was favored to win the Series in 1989. The ingredient the A's seemed to be missing for the world championship was a good leadoff batter.

With the A's, Rickey scored in 80 out of the 85 games he played in during the rest of the season. He led the league in stolen bases (77) for the ninth time in 10 seasons. He led off nine games with homers, giving him 40 leadoff home runs for his career and setting a new major league career record in that category. Rickey credited his "perfect eye at the plate" for his 126 walks, his highest number since arriving in the majors. New headlines appeared: "Best Leadoff Man Ever."

When the A's entered post-season play, Rickey said this was his "time to shine." His performance was dazzling. Against the Toronto Blue Jays in the American League Championship Series (ALCS), he got on base seven out of nine chances in the first two games. In the five-game series, he stole eight bases. His .400 batting average included two homers (in game three), as well as a double and a triple. He walked seven times, scored eight runs, and drove in five. The A's won the ALCS, and Rickey was named the most valuable player of the series.

For the first time in his 11-year career, Rickey Henderson was in the World Series. Henderson wasted no time getting started in the Series against Oakland's rival from across the San Francisco Bay, the Giants. He collected five hits in the first two games, although the A's could have gotten along without them. They easily beat the Giants, 5-0 and 5-1.

Just before game three was to start at Candlestick Park in San Francisco, an earthquake rocked the entire San Francisco-Oakland area. Because the earthquake had caused so much damage and killed more than 60 people, the World Series was postponed. When the Series was resumed 10 days later, Oakland hadn't lost a step. The A's won both game three and game four to sweep the World Series. Henderson had a magnificent showing. He hit .474 in the Series (including a leadoff homer in game four), stole three bases, and drove in three runs. In all of post-season play, Rickey stole 11 bases without once getting caught.

The MVP Season

As the 1990 season unfolded, the A's again were expected to dominate the American League Western Division and earn yet another trip to the World Series. Yet, as the A's rolled toward the last part of the season, most of the attention was on Rickey. Lou Brock's career record for stolen bases was within his reach.

The ball player who earlier in his career used raw speed to set new records on the base paths began talking about his skill as an art. "I call it an art because I studied all of them (great base stealers)," Rickey says. "I studied aggressiveness. I wanted to be a scientist—how many steps would it take me before I slide? That was based on Brock's style. Maury Wills sacrificed his body. I sacrifice my body too. . . . But I think of it as an art because when I get out there, I focus. My total concentration is focused on that moment when I'm going. I'm in a zone."

For most of the season, Rickey also led the league in hitting. But by September, George Brett had crept up on him, and Rickey was suddenly in a contest for the batting title. Near the end of the season, he admitted to *Sports Illustrated* that the batting title would be "the individual thing I'd like most," even though he was within a few steals of Brock's record. He knew he would soon have the base-stealing record. "It's going to come," he said. "I'm going to have the record. This isn't Rickey Henderson's final season." One goal was more important to him. "I want to make sure I'm 100 percent healthy for the play-offs and World Series."

Like Rickey did in hitting and base stealing, the A's also spent most of the season at the top. They had developed a reputation as an unbeatable team. In post-season play, while the Cincinnati Reds and the Pittsburgh Pirates battled for the National League Championship, the A's defeated the Boston Red Sox in four games. George Brett had beaten Rickey for the batting title. But for the third time in three years, the A's were headed for the World Series.

To almost everyone's surprise, Cincinnati's pitching and gritty play outmatched the A's hitting. The A's lost all four games they played in the World Series. Although some people questioned Oakland's desire in the World Series, no one could say that Rickey didn't try. He led his team in hitting (.300), including two doubles and a home run. He scored two runs, drove in a run, walked twice, and stole three bases without getting caught.

After the A's lost the first game, 7-0, game two began with a "Rickey rally." He led off with a single, stole second, took third on a sacrifice fly, and scored the A's first run of the Series. The game was tied 4-4 in the ninth. Playing left field, Rickey raced after a fly ball and just barely snagged it over his head in the web of his glove to save a run. Still, the A's lost 5-4 in the 10th inning.

Rickey, in a quiet moment, watches the game from the dugout.

In game three, with the A's trailing by five runs in the third inning, Rickey homered. He rounded first base, twiddling his hands in the air. Later, when he struck out, he muttered to himself all the way to the dugout. But no one criticized his style. No one claimed he was acting cocky. Instead, the television announcers praised him with respect and wonder for all he can do. When he did get on base, they even seemed to enjoy the way he flicked his fingers in his bright green gloves.

Shortly after the season ended, Rickey was named the American League's Most Valuable Player for 1990. He batted .325 and stole 65 bases. Cecil Fielder drew the second-most votes, hitting 51 home runs. But Rickey could do it all. He had worked his way from best base stealer to best leadoff batter. People seemed proud to say they watched one of the greatest baseball players who had ever lived.

RICKEY HENDERSON'S BASEBALL STATISTICS

Minor Leagues

Year	Team (class)	Games	Batting Average	At Bats	Hits	Runs	Home Runs	RBI	Walks	Stolen Bases
1976	Boise (A)	46	.336	140	47	34	3	23	33	29
1977	Modesto (A)	134	.345	481	166	120	11	69	104	95
1978	Jersey City (AA)	133	.310	455	141	81	0	34	83	81
1979	Ogden (AA)	71	.309	259	80	66	3	26	53	44
	Totals	384	.325	1335	434	301	17	152	273	249

Major Leagues

Year	Team	Games	Batting Average	At Bats	Hits	Runs	Home Runs	RBI	Walks	Stolen Bases
1979	Oakland	89	.274	351	96	49	1	26	34	33
1980	Oakland	158	.303	591	179	111	9	53	117	100
1981*	Oakland	108	.319	423	135	89	6	35	64	56
1982	Oakland	149	.267	536	143	119	10	51	116	130
1983	Oakland	145	.292	513	150	105	9	48	103	108
1984	Oakland	142	.293	502	147	113	16	58	86	66
1985	New York	143	.314	547	172	146	24	72	99	80
1986	New York	153	.263	608	160	130	28	74	89	87
1987	New York	95	.291	358	104	78	17	37	80	41
1988	New York	140	.305	554	169	118	6	50	82	93
1989	New York/Oakland	150	.274	541	148	113	12	57	126	77
1990	Oakland	136	.325	489	159	119	28	61	97	65
	Totals	1608	.293	6013	1762	1290	166	622	1093	936

*player's strike year

Major League Highlights:
American League Most Valuable Player, 1990
American League All-Star Team, 1980, 1982, 1983, 1984, 1985, 1986, 1987, 1988, 1990

Major League Records:
Most home runs as leadoff batter, lifetime (45)
Most years leading league in stolen bases (10)
Most times caught stealing, season (42—1982)
Most stolen bases, season (130—1982)
Most stolen bases, lifetime (939—as of May 1, 1991)

55

A happy Rickey Henderson answers questions at a press conference announcing his selection as the 1990 American League Most Valuable Player.

ACKNOWLEDGMENTS

Photographs are reproduced through permission of: pp. 1, 2, 17, Oakland Tribune/Gary Reyes; pp. 6, 8, 12, 46, Oakland Tribune/M. Macor; pp. 11, 14, Shmuel Thaler; pp. 19 (top), 35, 36, 44, UPI/Bettmann; p. 19 (bottom), Detroit Tigers; pp. 20, 21, Oakland Technical High School; pp. 22, 31, 34, 38, National Baseball Library; p. 24, The Associated Press; pp. 26, 32, Oakland Tribune/Ron Reisterer; p. 29, Oakland Tribune/Howard Erker; p. 41, Oakland Tribune/Angela Pancrazio; pp. 43, 48, New York Yankees; p. 53, Oakland Tribune/Pat Greenhouse; p. 56, Oakland Tribune/R. Pearman. Front and back cover photographs by Michael Zagaris.